# Which Will Win?

*To: Calli Yankee*
*May you hear from God through the messages in this book.*
*Sherry L. Gray*

## Sherry L. Gray

outskirts press

Which Will Win?
All Rights Reserved.
Copyright © 2021 Sherry L. Gray
v2.0

The opinions expressed in this manuscript are solely the opinions of the author and do not represent the opinions or thoughts of the publisher. The author has represented and warranted full ownership and/or legal right to publish all the materials in this book.

This book may not be reproduced, transmitted, or stored in whole or in part by any means, including graphic, electronic, or mechanical without the express written consent of the publisher except in the case of brief quotations embodied in critical articles and reviews.

Outskirts Press, Inc.
http://www.outskirtspress.com

ISBN: 978-1-9772-4475-8

Outskirts Press and the "OP" logo are trademarks belonging to Outskirts Press, Inc.

PRINTED IN THE UNITED STATES OF AMERICA

# Table of Contents

| | |
|---|---|
| DEDICATION | iv |
| 1. WHICH WILL WIN? FAITH OR DOUBT? | 1 |
| 2. KEEPING THE FAITH IS A LIFELONG JOURNEY | 9 |
| 3. TO CHEER AND NOT TO FEAR | 13 |
| 4. LOVE IN A FRAGILE WORLD | 17 |
| 5. WHO ARE WE IN CHRIST JESUS? | 21 |
| 6. JESUS IS THE SAME YESTERDAY, TODAY AND FOREVER | 25 |
| 7. YOU HAD SOMEONE DIE FOR YOU | 29 |
| CONCLUSION | 35 |

DEDICATION

TO

LOUIS L. GRAY

THE LOVE OF MY LIFE

MY BEST FRIEND

MY HUSBAND

AND

THE ONE I WILL STAND

BY HIS SIDE FOREVER

# WHICH WILL WIN?

## FAITH OR DOUBT ?!?!?!?!?!?!?!?!?!?!

# CHAPTER ONE

## WHICH WILL WIN? FAITH OR DOUBT?

Doubt is more pervasive than hate and more deadly than ignorance. Doubt of what GOD had said ultimately caused the first sin and separation from GOD. Adam and Eve did not believe eating the fruit of the tree of knowledge of good and evil that they would die. That is how serious doubt is. Adam and Eve were no longer innocent. They lived in shame of their bodies. They were naked. They hid yet as I believe GOD was always with them. HE knew what they had done. His heart was broken.

Satan tried to tempt JESUS after he had been led by the HOLY SPIRIT into the desert for 40 days. Satan suggest that JESUS throw HIMSELF down from the top of the temple in the HOLY CITY of Jerusalem, to harm HIMSELF or even worse to commit suicide?

We are bamboozled to think we do not matter or that our lives have no purpose nor hope. We live eat, sleep only if we have food or a place to lay down. There are those who do not have a place to lay their heads. They are out on the streets alone. They have no one to love them or help them. Some of them die and no one even knows who they are or where they came from. They merely exist and why because we doubt ourselves and the truth. Believing in nothing and have no faith has severe consequences. To be tempted to doubt is one thing. To live with disbelief is sin.

Our battles we face every day of

uncertainty demands our attention. Do we believe or do we doubt there is a way out? Either we believe what GOD says is true or HE is a liar. HE cannot contradict HIMSELF. We cannot please GOD without faith. That is why it is so important to trust GOD. It all starts with doubt. Doubt GOD'S existence. Doubt we have purpose. Doubt what we do really matters. Doubt GOD is love. Doubt GOD loves us. Doubt our salvation. Doubt GOD can heal, restore let alone give eternal life. Doubt cripples, divides, destroys, and takes away our joy, hope and meaning. That is what Satan wants us to focus on. Nothing miraculous can happen. GOD does not care about you. Or how about this, I guess I will quit? Or maybe even worse I will end it all? Whatever form of despair we face when doubt is behind it, it may be fatal. Faith on the other hand is powerful. A faith of a mustard seed can move a mountain.

When you trust by faith, there is actual a way out.

I was in the hospital with a rare parasite. The doctor told me that there was no cure for it. He said, "He would try something but doubt that the medication would work." I went to the door and yelled, "Get me out of here!" That next day I was ambulanced to University of Minnesota Fairview Hospital. I had been running to the bathroom 10-15 times a day. I was praying every time I went to the bathroom. One day I called a friend from Baltimore, Maryland. I had prayed with him, "GOD if it is my time for me to die, I am ready, no matter how I feel I trust you." "Whatever you have for me I receive it." I went to the bathroom and my stools were solid. That same day my husband Louis was riding a bicycle with only 10 pounds of air in his tires. He was thinking, "I am going to have to prepare a funeral for my wife." He got off his bike and said to himself. "No Satan, Sherry is going to be fine." "She is going to live." A peace came over him. He knew I was going to be alright. That afternoon I called Louis and left a message. The time was around 4 something the last day of July. I told him. "I went to the bathroom and my stools were solid." Louis was so happy he jumped up and clicked his heels in the air. That next day I went home.

On September 3rd, 2019, I went to the infectious disease doctor at Fairview Hospital in Minneapolis, Minnesota. She said, "You are cured." I could not stop asking her, "Are you sure?" She said, "Yes." Louis and I were so happy I cried and hugged Louis.

I am forever grateful for our family and friends that had prayed for us. It is the greatest thing on earth. Prayer does change things. I am alive because people believed what they prayed for.

We went home for our family reunion.

I was so glad I was able to see them. I did not die. I have an awesome life and I love my family as never before. All of them looked so good. I could have died had I believed the lie. There is a way.

Faith can heal I can attest to it. You will receive eternal life when, you repent and receive JESUS' forgiveness. What a contrast faith or doubt. Faith leads to eternal life and doubt will choke the life out of you. All of us are in the battle of war for our souls. We daily choose to believe GOD or doubt HIM. I choose rather to believe in hope and grow with JESUS through HIS SPIRIT.

Doubt is pervasive in the world today. JESUS knows our struggles with faith and doubt, that is why HE sent HIS SPIRIT. Our walk of faith does not have to be difficult, because JESUS has already, won the fight. HE has won the battle for our souls. We either doubt that or have faith and believe it. The truth remains GOD LOVES

YOU. Our decision to believe or disbelieve is a choice we all make. My question is, "Will you believe and have faith?"

When you trust JESUS the champion you will win eternally. Which will win, faith or doubt? It is all up to you.

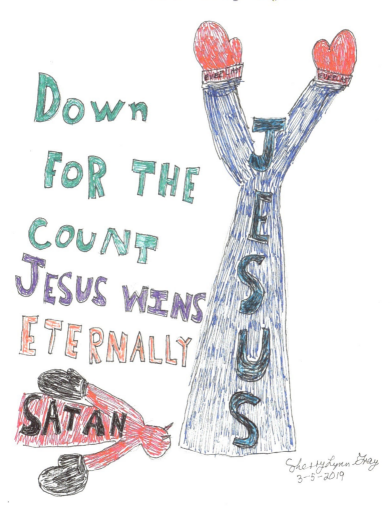

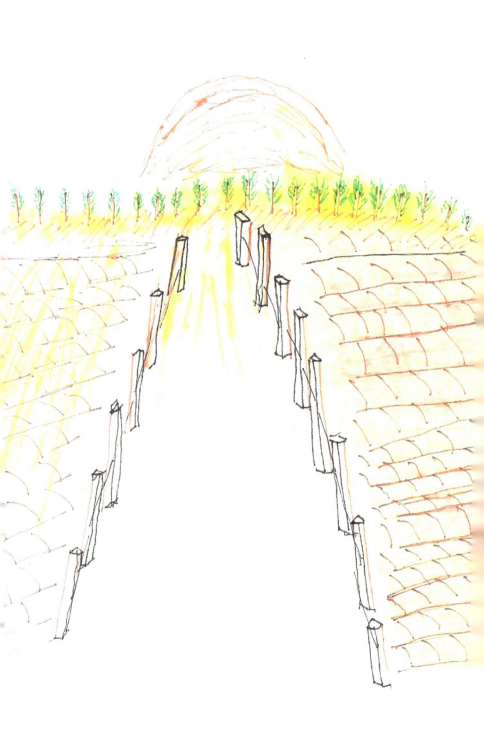

## CHAPTER TWO

# KEEPING THE FAITH IS A LIFELONG JOURNEY

THE POWER OF JESUS comes from HIS pureness, innocence, and total obedience of HIS HEAVENLY FATHER. There is a hunger in our souls that will not be satisfied. It is the void of GOD'S SPIRIT not living inside of us. Hunger for food, is not enough. There is more oh so much more. To live by the WORD OF GOD, is an everyday commitment. JESUS was guided by HIS HEAVENLY FATHER. HE also communes with us when we say, "Yes LORD."

Do you believe that you have no value, especially not with GOD? Do you believe you were a mistake? Do you question even the existence of GOD or that HE really, hears your prayers? We are tempted by our own doubts of GOD and a value of our own lives. Do you believe that GOD created something out of nothing? Miracles happen every day. We really are valuable.

The devil sometimes uses doubt into the mind of people from GOD'S existence to our salvation. But his fundamental objective is to cast doubt on the WORD OF GOD. Not believing it nor that we can act upon it. We are not sinning when we are oppressed by the temptation to doubt. Doubt only becomes sin when it is acted upon and allowed to control us. Satan tempted Adam and Eve to doubt GOD'S WORD. However, it was not until they did what he enticed them to do, that they had

sinned. Just because you are enticed to doubt does not mean that you have sinned. You can refuse to give into those suggestions. Faith and doubt are the real battle.
KEEPING THE FAITH IS A LIFELONG JOURNEY.

## CHAPTER THREE

―∽∽―

# TO CHEER AND NOT TO FEAR

JESUS HAD BEEN with HIS disciples by the sea of Galilee which is the sea of Tiberias. HE and the disciples were with thousands of people. 5,000 men plus women and children. It was late and people were hungry. Jesus was moved with compassion and fed them. HE blessed a few fish and loaves of bread and a miracle happened. They were all fed. After that JESUS perceived the people would take HIM by force because they wanted a king. JESUS straightway had to constrain the disciples to get to the ship and go to the other side while HE sent the thousands of people away. JESUS prayed in the mountains and when evening came, HE was alone.

While JESUS was in the mountains the disciples were in the middle of the sea of Tiberias 3.1 x 4.3 miles. They were frantically rowing because of a sea storm, the waves tossing, and wind was contrary. JESUS at the 4$^{th}$ watch of the night went to them, walking on the sea. All the disciples saw HIM walking on the sea. JESUS spoke to HIS disciples, "BE OF GOOD CHEER IT IS I JESUS."

When people, things, situations, are troubling us on every side, JESUS wants us to be of good cheer? Here is why we can be of good cheer. JESUS is our comfort in our times of storms. HE is the peace that surpasses understanding. JESUS hears us as we pray. JESUS heals, delivers, and restores people lives.

The 12 disciples rowed together yet the storms overtook them. Without JESUS everything else is too much to handle even with the 12 strong men. The storms overwhelmed them. Without JESUS we will be overwhelmed also. We need to call on JESUS to be rescued.

When I was younger, I had a very vivid dream. There were men and women inside of a block of ice. The ice block covered their entire bodies frozen. Other people there tried to free them with an axe and by their own strengths. The people that were picking away eventually got tired and quit. Someone asked, "Where is JESUS?" JESUS appeared where the people were frozen in the ice block. HE raised HIS hand toward the people and the ice block melted away and the people were set free.

How many times do we ask where is JESUS? Usually, it is when we are not aware that HE is right here with us. HE is helping us even when we do not recognize it. When we turn over our lives to JESUS, HE rescues us. This is the reason TO CHEER AND NOT FEAR.

## CHAPTER FOUR

# LOVE IN A FRAGILE WORLD

**JESUS IS THE** only pure LOVE that the world has ever seen, in a world of hate and HE died for it. HE understands the condition of people. HE understands loneliness, physical, mental, and emotional pain. HE understands abuse. HE understands neglect. HE understands abandonment. HE understands torture. HE understands death and gives us life. HE knows the enemy and JESUS is more powerful than him.

JESUS was there at the beginning of

time. HE is forever. HE is all that is good in the world. There is no darkness in HIM. HE is pure light. Yet HE had no place to rest HIS HEAD. HE created the universe. HE bled like we do. HE got blisters on HIS feet like we do. He would walk miles to meet people and connect with them. HE was moved with compassion to heal, deliver and even to raise people from the dead. JESUS, ALL POWERFUL, ALL KNOWING, AND EVERYWHERE AT ALL TIMES.

JESUS is LIFE itself. HE is the essence of true LIFE. HE understands everything we are going through. HE cares about us, LOVES us, and wants to help us. Why don't we let HIM? Why, are some of us so doubtful, stubborn, arrogant, proud, or so hateful? Without JESUS there is nothing good in us at all. Without JESUS there would be no LOVE and no forgiveness in a finite world.

Why do we continue to be selfish and self- sufficient? Why, do not we ask HIM to help us? That is my question to all of us.

JESUS experienced loss and lots of it. He lost friends. Even the 12 disciples had betrayed, denied, or left HIM. The exception is John who stood under the cross with JESUS' mother Mary, Mary Magdalene, and others when JESUS was crucified and died on the cross.

John took care of JESUS' mother Mary after JESUS had been crucified. JESUS understood John's commitment to LOVE. John loved to serve. To LOVE in a fragile world is to LOVE one another as we love ourselves. This is the new commandment JESUS asked us to follow.

## CHAPTER FIVE

# WHO ARE WE IN CHRIST JESUS?

**JESUS** WAS REJECTED by people in HIS hometown. HIS disciples ran and hid. Peter denied JESUS. JESUS was abandoned by the HEAVENLY FATHER, THE CREATOR OF ALL CREATION. HE called out to HIS HEAVENLY FATHER why have you forsaken me? HIS HEAVENLY FATHER had turned HIS BACK TO JESUS while HE was on the cross. HE was put to death by HIS peers. HE was tempted but never gave into it. HE had no place to lay his head.

People only wanted HIM for what HE could do for them. Religious leaders hated HIM and tried to entrap HIM. HE was a SERVANT, the ULTIMATE SERVANT. HE willingly laid down HIS life for all of us. HE intercedes to the HEAVENLY FATHER for us all. We will do more than HE did because HE left us the HOLY SPIRIT. HE asked HIS FATHER to forgive us. There was no forgiveness until HE died.

JESUS went through all we went through when HE died on the cross for all our sins. HE took all our sins for all of us no matter what we had done. Cursed is the man that hangs on a cross. JESUS knew no guilt but took all our guilt and curses on HIS body for us.

JESUS was born in a dirty feeding trough. HE worked with HIS hands. HE identifies with everyone. JESUS knows what is happening. HE knows how we think, choose, acts, and feels. HE loves us unconditionally with no strings attached.

I am in awe of what JESUS had done for all of us.

We give the devil to much credit. Who do we believe a temporary people or on an eternal GOD? WHO ARE WE IN CHRIST JESUS?

*CHAPTER SIX*

# JESUS IS THE SAME YESTERDAY, TODAY AND FOREVER

WHY DO PEOPLE see others suffer and watch but few want to help, or believe that they cannot, why? Where is their faith in GOD? He is making a way when there is no other way. Have we really understood what HE is doing? HIS LOVE has no end. HE is endless. He can broaden our hearts with HIS unconditional LOVE.

When hard times hit, HE will bring you through it. There are lessons you learn if you lean on the LORD. With pain, loss, or grief, GOD shows us even more how much we really need HIM.

Do we have opinions of others? Do we take the pain of our past and sometimes transfer it to someone else? For example, like a close friend or even a spouse, a family member, or a pastor, do we carry a grudge? No one knows what you have been through, and they are innocent. You do not see you are holding on to hurt nor do you want to see it. Your past still has hold of you! Let go and let GOD take you through the pain or loss or grief with HIS comforting presence. Nothing we will ever go through will take us from the unconditional LOVE of JESUS.

GOD does not take our problems away. HE helps us through them. JESUS even suffered loss. HE wept when HIS friend Lazarus died. The difference is HE raised him from the dead. JESUS is alive and HIS SPIRIT IS IN ME.

One day HE will come again. I pray

you will not be left behind. What I mean by that is JESUS went up to heaven in clouds over 2000 years ago. In the scriptures it says HE WILL RETURN FOR US IN CLOUDS OF GLORY. Are you ready for HIM?

JESUS IS STILL THE SAME YESTERDAY, TODAY AND FOREVER. HE completely accepts you just the way you are. HE paid for your sins, and HE will ALWAYS LOVE YOU! No matter what you do or do not do, HE will still LOVE you! HIS LOVE is ALWAYS AND FOREVER pure. HIS arms are open. Will you come into HIS embrace and let HIM LOVE you?

## CHAPTER SEVEN

# YOU HAD SOMEONE DIE FOR YOU

For **LOVE** sake I created you. I hear every cry, every whimper, every prayer you have ever prayed. I have been listening and know the desires in your heart. When you are in a mist or fog, I am there with you. I am there when you hurt or are in pain. I have answers you do not understand. When you look to ME, bear your soul. I know you and what consumes you. MY way is lighter. I carried those burdens, prayers, sorrows, whimpers, and cries to the cross with me. I carried them so you need not to. When you carry the burdens, then my dying means nothing to you. I understand and I still took your sins for you. Why do you hang on to your hurt or pain? I have a way that is best for you. Why dwell in the pain of the past? I have been there through it all with you. I will not force or push my way in. I am gentle, peaceful, and patient. You need ME. I am here for you.

Your sins all of them I took to the cross. I alone devote all MY LOVE and intentions for good and not to harm you. When you feed or pray or simply give a glass of water to someone who is thirsty, I am doing it through you. When someone sees someone hurting, abandoned, or wounded and helps them, MY heart of compassion is poured out. I am the way when there is no way. I can create something, from out of nothing there. I give life into a dying and hopeless world. I have you and I LOVE you. I created you. I knew you before you were born. I am here to heal, restore and set free those who are in spiritual bondage. Do you not know ME? I took all the beatings, abuse, and pain of the world on the cross. MY cross was for you. MY dying was to give you an abundant life. YOU ARE WORTH DYING FOR. MY mercies are new and fresh at every sunset and dawn. Every song the bird sings, every bend in a limb on a tree, every kitten's whimper for the mother's milk, and all around you I AM there. I AM the beauty of the universe. MY mercy keeps everything in space. The stars and planets are in MY merciful hands. I went to the cross. I carried all sins and curses on my body for you. YOU ARE WORTH DYING FOR. I did not stay there. So do not leave ME there. I will always give you victory when you obey ME. Trust me I will not fail you. I have made a way when there was no other way. What is impossible with people is possible with my HEAVENLY FATHER. There is none like HIM!

We all hope for an understanding of what is happening. Yet GOD in HIS SOVERN ways is waiting for us to look to HIM. When, we obey GOD, our lives are lighter and more joyful. When we disobey HIM, we carry the burdens that only HE can carry.

What an AWESOME AND MARVELOUS GOD we serve! HE made the trees, kittens, birds, planets, and stars! Yet in all HIS creations we were made to fellowship with HIM, and to be called HIS CHILDREN. Believe and call on the name of JESUS and you will be saved, saved from sin and death as we know it with no hope. No death but eternal life with no guilt nor condemnation.

When GOD THE FATHER looks at us, HE no longer sees our sins but HIS SON JESUS SPIRIT in us! Faultless and forgiven we are in CHRIST JESUS! Our part is to receive and trust all HE has for us.

GOD enters the praises of HIS CHILDREN. YES, WE ARE ALL WORTH

DYING FOR. Receive and believe it is true. HE is the way when there is no other way. YOU HAD SOMEONE DIE FOR YOU.

# CONCLUSION

**Which will win** faith or doubt? Which will win truths or lies? Which will win hope or hopelessness? Which will win joy or sorrow? Which will win comfort or confusion? Which will win eternity or mortality? Which will win saved or lost? Which will win free or captive? Which will win victor or victim? Which will win love or hate? Which will win cheer or fear? Which will helpful or helpless? Which will win innocent or guilty? Which will win accept or reject? Which will win courage or fear? Which will win durable or fragile? Which will win life or death?

These are the questions for your soul to ask, that the book has addressed. The choices we make are all up to us. No one is by themselves. GOD is everywhere. For some that might be frightening. To some it is a comfort. Each day we wake is an opportunity to make a difference. How we approach each day, will determine the outcome of our lives.

My question then is Which Will Win? Or should I ask, who will win? You or Jesus? HE is waiting for you to come to HIM. Will you come or will you resist? Life is in the balance for you. What will you do? Which Will Win?

CPSIA information can be obtained
at www.ICGtesting.com
Printed in the USA
BVHW020034140222
628944BV00001B/3